Table of Contents

T0052366

SHARED RESOURCES

CHAPTER 1

PLANNING AN INVASION

ith a storm tossing the seas, a tiny British submarine came to the water's surface off the coast of Normandy, France. It was late evening on June 5, 1944, and the minisub's five-man crew was tuning its radio to receive a coded message. The sub, called *X23*, was so small that the men had to take turns sleeping in its two bunks. They also worried if the bottles of oxygen that helped keep them alive would last until they completed their mission. The sailors waited to hear if they were going to take part in the largest amphibious assault ever attempted.

The Split History of the
D-DAY INVASION

ALLIES' PERSPECTIVE

BY MICHAEL BURGAN

CONTENT CONSULTANT:
G. Kurt Piehler, PhD
Associate Professor of History
Director, Institute on World War and the Human Experience
Florida State University

COMPASS POINT BOOKS
a capstone imprint

Compass Point Books are published by Capstone,
1710 Roe Crest Drive, North Mankato, Minnesota 56003
www.mycapstone.com

LIBRARY OF CONGRESS CATALOGING-IN-PUBLICATION DATA IS AVAILABLE ON THE LIBRARY
OF CONGRESS WEBSITE
    ISBN 9780756556907 (libary binding)
    ISBN 9780756568566 (paperback)
    ISBN 9780756556983 (eBook PDF)

Summary: Every battle has two sides, and the D-Day Invasion during World War II is no
different. Experience the event from perspective of the Allies, and then read the perspective of the
Germans. A deeper understanding of the battle from both sides will give readers a clearer view of
this historic event.

EDITOR
JENNIFER HUSTON

MEDIA RESEARCHER
TRACY CUMMINS

DESIGNER
HEIDI THOMPSON

PRODUCTION SPECIALIST
KATHY MCCOLLEY

The captain of an X-class minisub stands on deck giving orders to the crew just three weeks before the D-Day invasion. Minisubs played a key role in the attack.

The radio message came through; the attack was on. *X23* returned below the water's surface to avoid being detected by German ships or soldiers on land.

In the late 1930s, Germany had invaded large parts of Europe, including France. The amphibious assault planned for Normandy was designed to push the Germans out of the lands they had conquered and bring an end to World War II (1939–1945).

The crew of *X23* and another British minisub waited throughout the night. They had orders to surface again early on the morning of June 6. At that time, they would help guide British troops and tanks ashore, playing a key role in what the world knows today as D-Day.

A DREAM OF CONQUEST

World War II had started with Germany's invasion of Poland on September 1, 1939. German Chancellor Adolf Hitler had several goals in mind when he sent troops there and into other European countries. First, he wanted to make Germany the most powerful country in Europe. He also wanted to take back lands that Germany had been forced to give up after losing World War I (1914–1918). Hitler also wanted to rule over people who he considered inferior to Germans, such as the Poles. He believed Germans were superior to most other people and had a right to deny those people even their basic human rights. He particularly hated Jews, and anti-Semitism fueled many of his government's actions. Shortly after

Hitler's Nazi Party came to power in Germany in 1933, they passed laws that limited the freedom of Germany's Jewish citizens. Some were sent to prisons called concentration camps. As he conquered countries

Prisoners at concentration camps were given very little to eat. Two men in front are holding up a friend who is too weak to stand on his own.

across Europe, Hitler sent millions of European Jews to these camps. Some of the camps were "death camps." By the time World War II ended, the Germans had killed more than 6 million Jews — two-thirds of the entire Jewish population in Europe at the time.

Hitler also imprisoned non-Jewish people across Europe. Some were his political opponents. Others were from religious groups he didn't like. And some were imprisoned simply because they were physically or mentally disabled.

Great Britain and France declared war on Germany on September 3, 1939. These and other nations that fought Germany were called the Allies. The Soviet Union joined the Allies in June 1941. Germany and the countries that supported it, including Italy and Japan, were known as the Axis Powers.

At first, the United States did not send troops to the war front. After World War I, many Americans did not want to take part in another European war. Congress even passed laws that limited when the United States could help other countries at war. However, President Franklin Roosevelt saw the danger Hitler posed to the people of Europe and their freedom. In 1940 he convinced Congress to give the Allies weapons and military supplies.

The war finally came to the United States on December 7, 1941. On that day, waves of Japanese planes attacked U.S. naval ships stationed at Pearl Harbor in Hawaii. The next day, the United States declared war on Japan. On December 11, Hitler declared war on the United States. In the blink of an eye, the United States had been pulled into the deadliest war the world had ever known.

SEEKING A SECOND FRONT

By the end of 1941, Germany had conquered 11 countries in Europe, including France, which had surrendered in June 1940. A year later Germany launched an invasion of the Soviet Union. The fighting between the Germans and Soviets affected large parts of Eastern Europe, and the Soviets suffered heavy losses. The fighting in the east became the major European battlefront.

Soviet Premier Joseph Stalin urged Roosevelt and British Prime Minister Winston Churchill to open a second battlefront in Europe. Since June 1941, the Soviets had been fighting the majority of the German Army. By the end of the war, their casualties were in the millions. Stalin suggested an invasion of France, which would force the Germans to move some of their troops out of the Soviet Union. Roosevelt was on board, but Churchill had another idea: In late 1942, he suggested that the Allies first attack German-controlled lands in North Africa. From there, the Allies could attack Italy. As that fighting went on, the Allies could then start making plans for the amphibious invasion of France. They went forward with this revised plan of attack, and the invasion in France was given the code name Operation Overlord. Today, it is known as D-Day, which is a term used to describe a day on which an important event is planned.

PREPARING FOR OVERLORD

The Allies chose U.S. General Dwight D. Eisenhower to command the troops that would invade France. He had helped train troops during World War I. In 1942 and 1943, he commanded

General Dwight Eisenhower commanded the troops at Normandy and later became president of the United States.

U.S. troops that fought in North Africa and Italy.

Eisenhower received orders from the Combined Chiefs of Staff in February 1944 which said, "You will enter the continent of Europe and . . . undertake operations aimed at . . . Germany and the destruction of her armed forces." By early 1944 Eisenhower had nearly 3 million troops under his command. About half were American. The rest were mostly British and Canadian.

Leading up to D-Day, the Allies worked hard to deceive the Germans. They created fake plans for invading Norway, which Germany also controlled. They also wanted it to look like the attack would come at Pas-de-Calais, France, north of Normandy. The Allies sent out fake radio messages for the Germans to hear, describing an invasion force at Pas-de-Calais that didn't exist. They even built fake tanks and trucks out of rubber to trick German reconnaissance planes.

German spies who had been caught in England also helped the Allies. They agreed to work for the Allies rather than go to prison or be executed. These double agents helped spread false information about where the attack would occur and the size of the Allied forces.

ULTRA AND ENIGMA

The Allies had one way to measure how successful they were in deceiving the Germans. The Germans used a machine called Enigma to send coded messages, and the codes used changed daily. But in 1941 British mathematician Alan Turing was able to crack the code. Experts and an early computer helped Turing break Enigma's code and read the messages. The British called the information they gathered this way Ultra. By some estimates, cracking the Enigma code helped shorten the war by two years.

German soldiers used the Enigma machine to send coded messages.

Just before D-Day, the Allies learned the location of some underwater land mines the Germans had planted. With this information, the Allies could tell that the Germans believed the false information they had sent out.

During the buildup for Operation Overlord, the Allies kept their real intentions a secret. They built new airfields across England to use for the invasion. They hid supplies of ammunition in remote areas and brought in thousands of tanks and other vehicles. By May 1944 Eisenhower had decided the attack would come in June. He later wrote that the troops gathered in England were as "tense as a coiled spring . . . a great human spring coiled for the moment when its energy should be released."

CHAPTER 2

APPROACHING D-DAY

Eisenhower did not pick the date for Operation Overlord by chance. Weather, the tides, and the phases of the moon all played a part in the decision. Originally, the operation was planned for May, which would give the Allies more time to carry out their invasion during the warm summer months. Plus, Eisenhower knew that the Germans were building up their defenses along the Atlantic Coast in France to try to stop an amphibious invasion. Launching the attack in May would give them less time to do so.

However, Eisenhower decided to wait until June because he needed more time to build up the largest force possible for the attack. He decided the attack would come between June 5 and June 7. Those three days offered the best combination of a late-rising full moon and low tides. The late-rising full moon would give the first wave of troops more time to operate under darkness. The low tide would help the small landing craft carrying troops ashore avoid any obstacles the Germans had placed near the coast.

ALLIED ADVANTAGES

The switch from May to June also gave the Allies more time to use one of their huge military advantages—air power. In the weeks leading up to D-Day, bombers targeted German coastal defenses and artillery. They also destroyed bridges, railways, and trains so the Germans would have a hard time bringing reinforcements and supplies to Normandy.

By June 1 Allied bombing raids had destroyed almost all the bridges across the Seine, the major river that flows through northern France.

Members of the French Resistance set off explosives to destroy railroad tracks and sabotage the Nazis.

The Allies relied on help from the French Resistance—citizens who covertly operated against the Germans in support of the Allies by gathering information and carrying out sabotage. The Resistance cut telephone lines, which hindered communication for the Germans. Along railroad tracks the Resistance placed explosives, which they would set off when they received word of the invasion. A secret code sent by radio would alert them when the attack was about to begin.

THE JEDBURGHS

Both the British and Americans had organizations to spy and carry out secret missions behind enemy lines. For the British, the Special Operations Executive (SOE) did this work. For the Americans, it was the Office of Strategic Services (OSS). Together, members of the SOE and OSS worked with the French Resistance as part of special units called the Jedburghs. Each team usually included one British, American, and French member. On the night of June 5, the Jedburghs began parachuting into France and carried out sabotage to prevent the Germans from bringing reinforcements to Normandy, which aided the Allies in their ultimate victory on D-Day.

MAKING THE DECISION

With the information he had, Eisenhower chose June 5 for Operation Overlord. But ultimately, the weather would determine the day of the attack. If none of those days in early June worked, they would have to wait several weeks for the conditions they wanted. But a delay could be disastrous. If the Allies waited, the Germans could learn of the attack, and the element of surprise would be lost. Also, the Germans could strengthen their defenses and build new weapons. Waiting was not an option.

On June 4, Eisenhower and his staff met with chief meteorologist, Captain James Stagg. But Stagg didn't have good news. A storm was about to hit the coast of Normandy with strong winds and high waves that would make it difficult for the landing craft to safely reach shore. After some debate, Eisenhower decided to postpone the mission. Operation Overlord, or D-Day, would take place on June 6, weather permitting.

Early on the morning of June 5, Eisenhower once again met with his aides and Stagg. The meteorologist thought the weather would break long enough to launch the invasion the following day. Eisenhower decided it was worth the risk.

Some vessels, like the minisubs *X20* and *X25*, were already at sea. The men who would take part in the first wave of the assault got ready to join them. Between the airborne troops and those landing on shore, the Allies had a force of 156,000 men prepared to fight the Germans in Normandy. The Allies also had more than 7,000 ships and boats of all sizes ready for the invasion, along with almost 15,000 aircraft and gliders. Joining the U.S., British, and Canadian forces were troops from Australia, Belgium, Czechoslovakia, France, Greece, the Netherlands, New Zealand, Norway, and Poland.

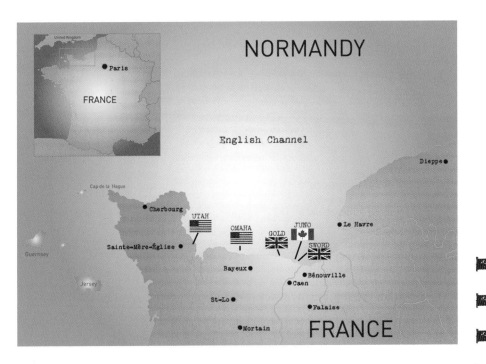

LAST-MINUTE PREPARATIONS

During the day on June 5, ships filled with soldiers began
leaving their docks and heading across the English Channel. Once
on the water, the seas were choppy, and many of the men got
seasick. On a British ship, William Seymour saw "waves coming
over the side of the ship. . . . But on we went, rocking from side
to side." Despite the rough crossing, many of the men knew they
had a mission to do. Alfred Leonard, a 16-year-old member of the
Merchant Navy, later said, "You were very aware that what was
about to happen was going to be important."

As they neared France, the men boarded smaller landing craft.
Then, they waded ashore at five beaches stretching 45 miles
(72 kilometers) along the Normandy coast. Each beach had its

own code name. The Americans were headed to Omaha and Utah beaches, the Canadians to Juno, and the British to Sword and Gold beaches.

While the ships moved toward France, 20,000 paratroopers prepared for their mission. Planes would take them past the German defenses on the shore so they could parachute farther inland. Their goal was to block important transportation routes so the Germans could not easily send reinforcements. Bomber crews got ready to take out German artillery before the land forces arrived. The huge operation required many pieces, and Eisenhower knew that the invasion could fail. On the night of June 5, he met some U.S. paratroopers just before they boarded their aircraft. He watched them take off for France and then went back to his camp. The outcome of D-Day was out of his control.

General Eisenhower has some encouraging words for Allied paratroopers before they leave to parachute into France.

CHAPTER 3

INVADING NORMANDY

*J*ust after midnight on June 6, as the troops on the ships prepared to storm the beaches of Normandy, 180 British commandos were already at work in France. Flying in six lightweight glider planes, they had quietly landed near the town of Bénouville. Their mission was to capture and hold two bridges in the region. British land forces would need to use those bridges once they came ashore.

With the element of surprise, the commandos quickly overwhelmed the bridges' defenders. In less than 20 minutes, the commandos had accomplished their mission.

Meanwhile, the first paratroopers began landing around the region. They carried packs weighing up to 100 pounds (45 kilograms) that were filled with weapons and supplies. But the landings didn't always go smoothly. Some paratroopers missed their targets. Others landed in trees and frantically cut off their parachutes before they could be captured by the Germans. In addition, the Germans had flooded some fields with water to make it difficult for the Allies to carry out an invasion. Under the weight of their heavy packs, some of the paratroopers drowned.

The thousands of paratroopers who landed safely began attacking German positions. American paratroopers were supposed to land outside the town of Sainte-Mère-Église, but some landed in the center of it and were quickly gunned down by the Germans. Others came upon French residents living near the town. Marcelle Hamel-Hateau saw a paratrooper land outside her house. He told her, "It's the big invasion . . . thousands of paratroopers are landing in this countryside tonight." Across Normandy, French residents like Hamel-Hateau welcomed the Allies' arrival.

APPROACHING THE BEACHES

Throughout the morning, Allied landing craft headed for the five target beaches. Meanwhile, more than 7,500 tons of bombs were dropped on German defensive positions along the coast. Some of the bombers also hit targets farther inland. The German air force had few planes in the region, so the Allied bombers flew with little resistance from German fighter planes.

The men in the landing craft watched as the Allied bombs sent dirt and smoke

British troops headed to Sword Beach on D-Day.

into the air. They counted on the planes to weaken the German defenses before their landing craft hit the beaches. Allied ships also fired their guns at the Germans waiting on shore. Author Ernest Hemingway was on one of the landing craft. He described how the boom of the giant naval guns shook the soldiers' helmets. The sound "struck your . . . ear like a punch with a heavy, dry glove."

In addition to troops, the British were also bringing ashore some amphibious tanks that could advance through shallow water as well as roll on land. They also had tanks called "funnies" that were designed to carry out special duties. Some shot flames almost 400 feet (122 m). Others had revolving barrels in the front that could explode land mines the Germans had buried in the sand.

The Germans had also placed land mines and obstacles in the water. Huge steel frames called Belgian gates formed a wall off the coast. Other obstacles, called hedgehogs, had crossed steel beams up to 5 feet (1.5 m) tall. Some obstacles also had land mines attached to them. Specially trained teams of sailors had the job of blowing up the obstacles before the landing craft reached them. Along with U.S. Army engineers, they were supposed to clear paths 50 feet (15 m) wide. These sailors were nicknamed "frogmen" because they originally wore green rubber suits in the water.

As the Allied landing craft approached the beaches, the Germans on shore began firing back. The frogmen worked as bullets whizzed by their heads. Meanwhile, some landing craft were tossed by the rough seas into obstacles and land mines that hadn't been destroyed. Some troops landed in the water without their weapons and tried to swim ashore as the Germans fired at them. Along the five beaches, the Allied troops began to realize that the bombing raids and naval guns had not destroyed as much of the German defenses as Eisenhower had hoped.

ACTION ON THE BEACHES

At 6:30 a.m. the first troops came ashore at Omaha and Utah beaches. Additional troops began hitting the other three beaches soon after. Some men drowned in the rough waters before they could reach the shore. Others were hit by German gunfire. Medics came to the aid of the wounded and dying who screamed for help.

Meanwhile, additional U.S. soldiers kept pouring out of the landing craft. Once on shore, they tried to take cover behind obstacles or small rocks. Some dodged minefields to approach the German defenses. Their goal was to get close enough to toss hand grenades inside and take out the Germans manning the machine guns. But enemy gunfire was also coming from the cliffs above the beaches. U.S. naval ships moved closer to shore to try to knock out the German defenses, while thousands of men continued to storm the beaches. As one U.S. infantry unit reported, "The enemy now began to pour artillery and mortar fire on to the [crowded] beach with deadly precision and effect." The fighting at Omaha Beach was the bloodiest of the day, with an estimated 3,686 casualties compared to 4,158 at the other four beaches combined.

The beaches where the Allies landed on D-Day spanned a 45-mile (72-km) stretch.

The landing at Utah Beach started poorly with the troops missing their planned target, but the mistake turned into an advantage. German defenses were lighter there than at the planned landing spot, so the American troops quickly came ashore. At Omaha Beach, the rough water had sank most of the amphibious tanks before they reached shore, but more of them made it at Utah Beach. The coast there also had fewer obstacles. The next waves of incoming troops headed for the same spot rather than the original target. They came ashore with little German resistance.

The British and Canadians had an easier time landing on the beaches than the Americans. Still, at times they faced fierce fighting. At Gold Beach, British troops battled all day to establish a firm position on the beach. British soldier Ken Coney, who came ashore that morning, later wrote in his diary, "Dead and dying are everywhere. I can't understand why I am not frightened." At Sword Beach, British and French troops needed less than an hour to move inland and reach their first target.

BACK IN ENGLAND

As the fighting raged throughout the morning, Eisenhower waited for news. He had already written a message he would send to the world if the invasion failed. It said in part, "If any blame or fault attaches to the attempt, it is mine alone." But as the attack went on, he was pleased with the reports he heard. At 10 a.m. the British Broadcasting Company (BBC) played a message that Eisenhower had recorded earlier. It began, "People of Western

D-Day was an enormous undertaking that involved 156,000 Allied troops, 7,000 ships and landing craft, 11,000 aircraft, and 13,000 paratroopers.

Europe: a landing was made this morning on the coast of France. . . . This landing is part of the . . . United Nations plan for the liberation of Europe, made [together] with our great Russian allies. I have this message for all of you. Although the initial assault may not have been made in your own country, the hour of your liberation is approaching."

However, by the end of the day, the Allies had not met all of their goals. The British and Canadian forces had not taken the town of Bayeux or the city of Caen as Eisenhower and his staff had hoped. And there were still gaps along the beaches between the various Allied forces. But the Allies had managed to bring more than 150,000 men ashore. Ultimately, D-Day was a success for the Allies, but the fighting was far from over.

A REAL PRIVATE RYAN

The 1998 movie *Saving Private Ryan* shows the death
and destruction of D-Day in gruesome detail.
The movie also tells the story of a group of
U.S. soldiers who take on a dangerous mission
behind German lines. They're sent to find and
bring home a paratrooper after his brothers
were killed in battle.

The plot is similar to a real-life story that
occurred after D-Day. Frederick "Fritz" Niland
was one of four brothers who served during World
War II. Fritz took part in the Normandy invasion,
but in July, he was ordered home because his
three brothers were believed to have been killed
in battle. (One was actually in a Japanese
prisoner-of-war camp and later managed to escape.)
President Roosevelt had earlier said that no
American family should lose more than two sons
during the war. When Niland heard he was going
to be sent home, at first he refused, but he
eventually followed orders and returned home.

CHAPTER 4

AFTER D-DAY

On June 7, General Eisenhower talked with his generals in Normandy. Although the Allies had successfully landed on all five beaches, some German forces remained in the area and continued to fire artillery at the Allies.

While the first Allied troops to land on Normandy pushed inland, more came ashore. The goal was to link the five beachheads into one solid line of Allied troops and weapons. That would prevent the Germans from trying to attack through any gaps in the line. Then the Allies could safely bring ashore all the supplies and weapons they would need to push their way into the heart of France.

THE FIGHTING GOES ON

The number of Allied casualties on D-Day is hard to pin down, but historians place it around 11,000. This includes an estimated 4,400 Allied troops killed on the beaches during the invasion. Also included in the number of casualties are those who were taken prisoner—mostly paratroopers or pilots whose planes were shot down. The number of casualties continued to grow in the weeks that followed, but the Allies managed to gain more ground.

The Germans put up a stiff defense around Caen, and their reinforcements began to arrive from other parts of France. The Germans also used planes to drop land mines off the coast to slow the Allies' efforts to bring in more men and supplies. Specially designed Allied ships "swept" the waters of the land mines.

Eisenhower called these first few weeks of fighting in Normandy "the Battle of the Beachhead." The Allies gained ground slowly, but as Eisenhower later wrote, "It was during this period that the stage was set for the later, spectacular liberation of France and Belgium." During this time, the Allies began moving ashore more than 2 million troops that would carry out that liberation.

The Allies maintained their superior air power, which made it difficult for the Germans to move reinforcements to the front. The Allies also continued to rely on the French Resistance and Jedburgh teams to sabotage and slow down the Germans. And in the first days after D-Day, the Allies kept sending fake messages to deceive the Germans. Those messages convinced Hitler and some of his generals that another attack was still to come.

By the end of July, the British and Canadians had driven the Germans out of Caen. The fighting there was particularly heavy, with several hundred Allied tanks destroyed. Even so, the Allied invasion of France was under way with a goal to not just push back the Germans but also close in on them and destroy as much of their army as possible.

The Germans launched counterattacks when they could, including one in early August near Mortain. Against U.S. forces led by General George Patton, the Germans initially advanced, but they were soon pushed back. The Allies then circled the German troops near Falaise, killing about 10,000 and capturing 50,000 others.

THE SECOND INVASION

As the fighting went on around Mortain and Falaise, the Allies launched a second amphibious assault on France. On August 15, they came ashore on the Mediterranean coast in the south of France. As at Normandy, they relied on paratroopers, planes, and naval guns to begin the attack. German defenses were much weaker in southern France than they had been at Normandy. French forces quickly took control of the port city of Marseille, and U.S. troops headed north along the Rhône River. By September, the Americans united with Allied forces pushing east from Normandy, and together they advanced toward the German border.

By then, the Allies had liberated Paris from the Germans. For more than four years, the city's residents had been under German rule. In late August, as the Allies approached the city, the German troops surrendered. Soon, a million joyful Parisians filled the streets to welcome the Allies.

Throughout the rest of 1944 and into the spring of 1945, the Allies continued their push eastward toward Germany. But there were some setbacks along the way. A September operation in the Netherlands called Market Garden ended in failure. British and American paratroopers were supposed to take several bridges across the Rhine River to make it easier for ground forces to invade Germany. However, the Germans had experienced troops in the area, and they held off the attack. Then, in December, the Germans launched their last great counterattack, known as the Battle of the Bulge. During the fighting in the forests of Belgium, the Germans inflicted heavy losses on the Allies, but they also lost 80,000 men in the process. All this went on as Soviet troops continued to fight German forces in Eastern Europe.

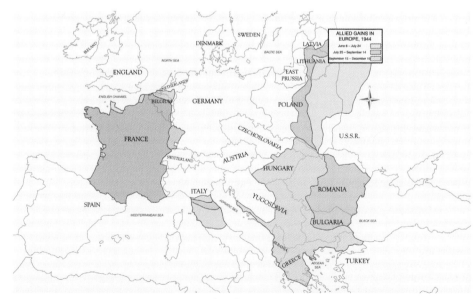

D-Day was a turning point for the Allies in World War II. After the invasion, the Allies took back much of the land that the Nazis had taken over.

The spring of 1945 saw the Allies moving toward the German capital of Berlin from two sides. The Soviets advanced from the east, while the British and American forces came from the west. The Soviets reached Berlin first and began bombarding the city on April 20, Hitler's birthday. Ten days later, Hitler committed suicide, and on May 8, Germany officially surrendered. Although fighting continued in some parts of Europe and Asia, the war against the Nazis was over.

FINAL VICTORY

After D-Day, it took the Allies less than a year to defeat Nazi Germany. Without the successful landing at Normandy, the Allies could not have amassed the huge force they needed to push back the Germans. Eisenhower believed the Allies' superior air power and the Germans' lack of good intelligence about what the Allies planned to do were largely responsible for achieving this goal.

In writing his report on the fighting in Europe, Eisenhower also noted the important role civilians played in producing all the weapons and equipment the troops used. He wrote, "No army or navy was ever supported so generously or so well. Never . . . were we forced to fight a major battle without the weapons that were needed."

Although the massive D-Day invasion took place decades ago, the world still remembers the bravery and courage the troops showed in one of the most important battles in world history.

INDEX